Brussels in 3 Days:

The Definitive Tourist Guide Book That Helps You Travel Smart and Save Time

Book Description

Why is Brussels in 3 Days the best Brussels travel guide for you?

If you want a travel guide that's easy to read, with up-to-date information, look no further. You can follow the rest of the tourists and visit the most famous attractions in Brussels, but there are so many popular attractions. We help you sort them out, so you can hit the ones you want in a three-day vacation. We'll also show you some hidden gems that are a bit off the tourist maps.

Use this guide to plan your trip. We have highly-rated ("very good" or higher) hotels in three price ranges, and we list the closest attractions to each hotel, so you can choose one that will be convenient for you.

This guide is perfect if you've never before visited the "capital of Europe". We give you the information you'll need to get to town from the airport, and then around town, once you're there.

Are you a foodie? Even if you're not, you'll enjoy perusing our restaurant section, split by price points and offering many types of cuisine.

If you only have a few days to spend in Brussels, this guide is the perfect choice. Plan and enjoy your trip with the best information at your fingertips.

The People of Brussels
The region around Brussels is quite urbanized. The population of the capital region is about 1.2 million. Many people move to the area every year. The population of the city is younger than Belgium's national average.

People with foreign origins make up almost 70% of Brussels' population. Most were nationalized after the 1991 reform of Belgium's naturalization process. About one-third of Brussels residents are of European origin, but not from Belgium. More than one-third have other backgrounds, most being from Sub-Saharan Africa, Morocco and Turkey.

Belgians have a famously good sense of humor. They are not overtly welcoming to foreigners, but those in the tourist industry have a vested interest in being more than hospitable to visitors. The country is gay-friendly and open, and among the most modernized populations worldwide.

Language

Brussels has many foreign-speaking people who call the city home. In 2013, figures showed that over 60% of inhabitants of Brussels are native French speakers. Fewer than 20% speak Dutch as their native tongue. Less than 3% have English as a mother tongue, but almost 30% of Brussels residents speak English at least fairly well. Dutch is the legal language, but French is used a great deal, and much signage, menus, etc., include both Dutch and French.

The migrants, whose communities are growing rapidly in Brussels, speak many languages. They include Turkish, French, Berber, Arabic, Italian, Spanish, German, Polish, Portuguese and English.

Holidays

Jan 1	New Year's Day	National holiday
March	March equinox	Season
April	Good Friday	Observance
April	Easter Day	National holiday
April	Easter Monday	National holiday
May 1	Labor Day/May Day	National holiday
May	Ascension Day	National holiday
June	Whit Sunday	National holiday
June	Whit Monday	National holiday
June	June Solstice	Season
July	Belgian National Day	National holiday
August	Assumption of Mary	National holiday
Sep	September equinox	Season
Nov 1	All Saints' Day	National holiday
Nov 11	Armistice Day	National holiday
December	December Solstice	Season
Dec 24	Christmas Eve	Observance
Dec 25	Christmas Day	National holiday
Dec 31	New Year's Eve	Observance

Religious Beliefs

Belgium has freedom of religion, and separation between Church and State. The government can't force people to adhere to or abstain from practicing any religion.

The 2013 Belgian census did not ask residents their religion, which has made it more difficult when it comes to pinpointing the percentage of each religion in Belgium. An independent report done recently shows that about 62% of Belgians adhere to Christianity, in some form. Almost 60% identify themselves as Roman Catholic. Two percent of Belgians identify themselves as Protestant (over 1.5%) or Orthodox (0.3%).

Behind Christianity, the largest religion practiced in Belgium is Islam, which accounts for six to eight percent of their population. Most Muslims live in the Brussels area. There are about 40,000 Jews in Belgium, and 21,000 Anglicans. There are some other religions represented in Belgium, too. They include Mormonism, Jehovah's Witnesses, Hinduism, Jainism, Sikhism and Buddhism.

Here is a quick preview of what you will learn in this tourist guide:

- Helpful information about Brussels
- Flying into the city
- Transportation tips in town
- Why Brussels is such a vibrant tourist spot and what you will find most remarkable about it
- Information on luxury and budget accommodations and what you'll get for your money
- The currency used in Brussels
- Tourist attractions you should make time to see
- Other attractions for entertainment and culture
- Events that may be running during your stay
- Tips on the best places to eat & drink for all price points, whether you want simple fare, worldwide dishes or Belgian flavor

Table of Contents

Introduction 1
1. Key Information about Brussels 8
2. Transport to and in Brussels 10
3. Accommodations 16
4. Sightseeing 23
5. Eat & Drink 27
6. Culture and Entertainment 34
7. Special Events in Brussels 38
8. Safety in Brussels 42
Conclusion 44

Introduction

Brussels is quite a cosmopolitan city, holding an appeal and liveliness that come from its role as the crossroads of Europe. Styles of architecture include classic facades like that of the Palais des Nations and the Gothic style of many churches and cathedrals.

Brussels is home to Grand Place, which holds splendid restaurants and sidewalk cafes. The charming cobblestone streets will take you to such attractions as the Town Hall, King's House and the well-known statue Mannekin Pis, which almost doesn't need translation, once you see it.

Brussels is also home to up-market shopping areas, major museums and the Belgian Parliament Building. The city and its surrounding region offer many interesting attractions. Brussels itself is compact and small, but some of its best attractions lie on the outskirts of the city.

A Brief History of Brussels

Brussels was founded officially by the Duke of Low Lotharingia, in 979. He established the first city charter. Brussels has seen many rulers, revolutions and renaissances since that time.

979 – 1500: The Middle Ages

After its founding, Brussels quickly developed from a small town to a larger city. Even then, it was the trade center for the cities of Cologne, Bruges and Ghent. In the 1000's, city walls were finished and this protection led to additional population growth. Brussels was the Duchy of Brabant capital city in the 1300s, 1400s and 1500s.

At its earliest economic height, luxury items were exported from Brussels. They included tapestries and fabrics, and were shipped to Venice and Paris. In the 1400s, the King's House and Town Hall were built, rising over the Old Town at Grand Place.

1500 – 1830: Renaissance and Revolution

This period was marked by uprisings and rebellions. After an uprising against Roman Emperor Maximilian I, Brussels lost its capital status. The status was regained when Charles V took over between 1519 and 1559.

The Grand Place was left in ruins after a bombardment of the city by France's King Louis XIV in 1695. The city had buildings torn to the ground in many areas. Brussels was rebuilt by craftsmen, and in the remainder of the 1700s, the city was the center of not just economic development, but also revolts. The current Brussels status of capital city was established with the independence of Belgium in 1830.

1830 – present: Modern history

The last major revolt in Belgium occurred in 1830. At this time, the people protested Netherland's King William and achieved their independence. The first King of Belgium was Leopold I, named on July 21, 1831.

The city's walls were removed in the years following the last large revolt, replaced with boulevards shaped into a pentagon. The same road is traveled by the current Circle Metro Line. By 1846, the population of Brussels was 123,000.

The 1900s were not only a period of war, but also of development. After WW I and WW II, Germany occupied Brussels, and the Brussels Pact in 1948 led to the formation of the Western European defense commitments. The European Union (EU) is still an economic cooperation, and still developing today.

The first metro lines in Brussels were built in the 1960s, helping to ease the urban congestion. In the 1970s and the 1980s, political reform was responsible for the creation of the Brussels Capital Region. This expanded the city to include its surrounding areas, and the population after this act was over one million.

Neighborhoods

The Lower Town

This is the core of the Old Center, with Grand Place at its heart. The area contains the Stock Exchange, the Monnaie Opera House & Ballet Theater. The busiest street for shopping is also found here, the pedestrianized rue Neuve.

The Upper Town

This area is uphill from and to the east of Grand Place. You'll find bars and cozy cafes in this neighborhood. It is home to the Royal Museum of Fine Arts and the museums of the Place Royal.

European District

This area lies east of the center of the city. It is the neighborhood that holds the Council of Ministers, the European Commission and Parliament, all parts of the EU district. There are many cafes and restaurants in this area, too.

Avenue Louise

This street runs south to a large park, known as Bois de la Cambre. On both sides of Avenue Louise, you will find shopping, cafes, bars and restaurants, most of them inexpensive.

Bruparck

This neighborhood plays host to Brussels' recreation area. It is home to the Oceade Water Park, the Mini-Europe theme park and the Kinepolis movie theater. Nearby you will find the Brussels Planetarium, Atomium, the Parc des Expositions congress center and the Roi Baudoin Soccer Stadium.

What does Brussels offer its Visitors?

Brussels is an unassuming city, yet it is the capital of not only Belgium, but also Flanders and Europe. The flower markets and 17th-century buildings are favorite places for travelers to visit.

Atomium is known as Brussels' Eiffel Tower, and provides wonderful views, both inside and outside. Fans of architecture will find many interesting buildings, including Museum Horta. The bars and clubs of St. Gery's are busy year-round, and Ste. Catherines abounds with seafood eateries. It's easier to walk than drive in the city's narrow streets.

1. Key Information about Brussels

Money Matters

Belgium is a member country of the European Union and uses the euro as its currency. The euro is sun-divided into 100 euro cents.

Notes are issued in denominations of €5, €10, €20, €50, €100, €200 and €500. Each note has a color all its own.

Coins are issued in 1 cent, 2 cents, 5 cents, 10 cents, 20 cents, 50 cents, €1 and €2 denominations.

As you arrive in Brussels, exchange your traveler's checks or currency at a local bank, rather than an exchange bureau, shop or hotel, since those have higher commissions and rates. In addition, most of the local hotels accept major branded credit and debit cards.

Tipping

Tipping is not typically common in Brussels, or Belgium as a whole. Taxi and restaurant bills already include a service charge. Service and wait staff in Brussels are better paid than their US counterparts, so they don't have to rely on tips as a vital part of their income.

If you receive outstanding service somewhere, you can round up your bill or leave a few Euros. In some of Brussels' more touristy places, the staff may expect a tip, but you are not obligated to leave them one.

Tipping the staff at your hotel is also uncommon, since your bill total includes services. You can leave the bellman a couple euros, if you wish to. Customer service workers and housekeepers are not customarily tipped.

Restaurant Tipping

You're not expected to tip in restaurants, since the service charge has been added to your bill. If you had exceptional service, you can leave a few extra euros, but you don't have to.

2. Transport to and in Brussels

Getting to Brussels by Plane
Brussels Airport serves the Brussels region in Belgium. It's about seven miles northeast of the city. More than 23 million passengers flew in or out of Brussels airport in 2015.

Getting to Brussels from the Airport

Brussels Airport bus service
You'll find the bus station on level 0, which is one level down from the arrival hall. There are elevators or escalators for reaching the lower level. There are three platforms located centrally at the bus station.

Brussels Railway airport service
The airport's railway station is found at level -1, under the main airport building. It has direct service to Brussels and other Belgian cities. The most often used link, to Brussels, has at least four trains arriving and departing per hour.

Brussels Rental Cars

There are several car rental companies at the airport. They include Thrifty, Sixt, Hertz and Europcar. If you're only visiting Brussels, and no other cities, you probably won't need to rent a car. Most of the attractions are accessible by foot and mass transit.

Brussels Cabs

The airport is an easy place to get taxis. They are also available in train stations, on large avenues and at the entrances to larger hotels. They don't have a special color to distinguish them from regular cars, but they do have signs on the roof, designating them as taxis.

Payment and Tipping for Taxi's

Taxis have a daytime minimum charge of $2.74 and a night minimum charge of $4.80. The exact price for your trip will be displayed on the taxi meter, and it includes a service charge.

There are Roman numerals on the signs on taxi roofs, either I or II. The "I" taxis stay in central Brussels and "II" taxis travel the perimeter.

Because of the fare structure and who collects the tariffs on taxi service, it is usually more expensive to get from the airport TO the city than the trip back to the airport.

Do not accept taxi rides from drivers who offer you a ride outside the airport and not in the taxi queue. Go to the official taxi queue. If you want to pay for your taxi trip with a credit card, this is an option in some, but not all, taxis. Ask before you take off.

You are not expected to tip taxi drivers, but you may leave the change for them, and round your charge up to the next euro. If your driver is especially helpful with bags or directions, you can leave a tip. Just a few euros are sufficient.

Public Transport in Brussels

Brussels Underground Metro

Brussels' underground train is a fast and convenient way to travel to the main tourist destinations in the center of the city. Four metro lines serve the center of the city. They run quite frequently. During peak hours, they run every three minutes. On the weekends, they run every five minutes, and after 8 PM any night, every 10 minutes.

Metro and tram doors don't open automatically, so you'll need to push a button or pull a lever when they stop at your desired stop.

To make it easier to orient yourself at local metro stations, look for info symbols when you get on or off the train. There is a map of the street above you, and it can be used to determine what exit to take. They are also found at bus and tram stops, and are useful for travelers.

At most metro platforms and stations, you will find machines for prepaid mobile recharges, drinks and snacks.

Brussels Bus

Buses may be more convenient for you if your departure location or your destination aren't close to metro stations. Bus timetables are posted at each stop. They don't run as frequently as metro trains.

You can purchase tickets from bus drivers for 2 euros ($2.28 USD) for a one hour jump ticket, useable for trams and the metro as well. It is cheaper to buy tickets at metro stations.

Brussels Tram

Tram service is similar to that of metro and bus, but they are slower than metro trains and arrive more frequently than buses. Trams run along streets, and sometimes on the line used by cars, if there isn't enough space on the narrow roads. Watch for trams and cars whenever you cross the street. Arrival and departure times and stops can be seen at each tram stop. There are street maps at all stops, too.

Passes & Tickets

Public transport in the inner city of Brussels uses unified tickets. The same ticket works for buses, metro, trams or any combination. As a tourist, the one day tickets are probably your best choice, since the other options are for monthly use.

You can buy tickets at GO machines at metro stations. They must be validated at the small machines seen before you get on the metro. Non-validated cards will result in fines.

3. Accommodations

There are all kinds of hotels and other choices like Air B&B's available in Brussels. They are a bit pricier than those of less popular tourist areas, but fairly close in price to those in other major European cities.

Prices for luxury hotels:
$400 - $645 USD per night

Rocco Forte Hotel Amigo
- Close to Lower Town, Mannekin Pis Statue, Grand Place, Church of Our Blessed Lady of the Sablon, Cathedral of St. Michael

Hilton Brussels Grand Place
- Close to Upper Town, Brussels Park, Grand Place, Cathedral of St. Michael, Place Royale

Tangla Hotel Brussels
- Close to the European Union Parliament Building, Autoworld Museum, Confederate Museum, Woluwe Shopping Center, NATO Headquarters

The Hotel
- Close to Grand Place, Mannekin Pis, Museum of Musical Instruments, Royal Museums of Fine Arts, Church of Our Blessed Lady of the Sablon

Aloft Brussels Schuman
- Close to European Quarter, Church of Our Blessed Lady of the Sablon, Cathedral of St. Michael, Royal Museums of Fine Arts of Belgium, Museum of Musical Instruments, European Union Parliament Building

Radisson Blu Royal Hotel
- Close to Lower Town, Mannekin Pis Statue, Grand Place, Cathedral of St. Michael

Eurostars Montgomery
- Close to Belgian Comic Strip Center, Royal Museums of Fine Arts, Cathedral of St. Michael, Museum of Musical Instruments, European Union Parliament Building

Prices for mid-range hotels: $195 to $300 USD per night

Beau Séjour Appart Bruxelles
- Close to Lower Town, Grand Place, Mannekin Pis Statue, Museum of Musical Instruments, Cathedral of St. Michael, Church of Our Blessed Lady of the Sablon

Hilton Garden Inn Brussels Louise
- Close to Manneken Pis Statue, Horta Museum, Royal Museums of Fine Arts, Museum of Musical Instruments, Church of Our Blessed Lady of the Sablon

The Pantone Hotel
- Close to the Heart of Brussels, Manneken Pis Statue, Museum of Musical Instruments, Royal Museums of Fine Arts, Church of Our Blessed Lady of the Sablon, Horta Museum

The Vintage Hotel

- Close to the Heart of Brussels, Manneken Pis Statue, Museum of Musical Instruments, Royal Museums of Fine Arts of Belgium, Horta Museum, Church of Our Blessed Lady of the Sablon

Citadines Toison d'Or Brussels
- Close to Manneken Pis Statue, Horta Museum, Museum of Musical Instruments, Royal Museums of Fine Arts of Belgium, Church of Our Blessed Lady of the Sablon

MAS Residence
- Close to European Quarter, Cathedral of St. Michael, Royal Palace of Brussels. Berlaymont Building

Residence Agenda
- Close to Heart of Brussels, Royal Museums of Fine Arts of Belgium, Horta Museum, European Union Parliament Building, Museum of Musical Instruments, Church of Our Blessed Lady of the Sablon

Prices for inexpensive hotels: $150 USD per night and less

Hotel Phenix
- Close to Grand Place, Mannekin Pis Statue, Church of Our Blessed Lady of the Sablon, Cathedral of St. Michael, Constant Vanden Stock Stadium

City Center Apartments Fourche
- Close to Lower Town, Belgian Comic Strip Center, Manneken Pis Statue, Cathedral of St. Michael, Grand Place

Best Western County House of Brussels
- Close to Van Buuren Museum, Horta Museum, Museum of Musical Instruments, Royal Museums of Fine Arts, Church of Our Blessed Lady of the Sablon

Hôtel Van Belle
- Close to Grand Place, Mannekin Pis Statue, Museum of Musical Instruments, Cathedral of St. Michael, Church of Our Blessed Lady of the Sablon

Aparthotel Résidence Bara Midi
- Close to Grand Place, Mannekin Pis Statue, Royal Museums of Fine Arts of Belgium, Church of Our Blessed Lady of the Sablon, Museum of Musical Instruments

Condo Gardens Brussels
- Close to Grand Place, Belgian Comic Strip Center, Manneken Pis Statue, Cathedral of St. Michael, Museum of Musical Instruments

Urban Suites Brussels EU
- Close to Upper Town, Royal Museums of Fine Arts of Belgium, Museum of Musical Instruments, Belgian Comic Strip Center, Cathedral of St. Michael, European Union Parliament Building

Airbnb's

For just $20 USD per night, you can rent a large private room in a Brussels apartment. It's close to major tram and bus stops, 20 minutes from the airport and 10 minutes from the Brussels-North Railway Station. You'll also be within 15 minutes of the heart of Brussels. There is a bar, supermarket and bakery close by, too.

$145 USD per night rents you a smartflat in a warm, welcoming residence just a few steps from the shops of Avenue de la Toison d'Or. There is easy access to the heart of historic Brussels. The room is modern, with double beds. It has a private bath and is located on the second floor of a building with no elevator.

You can rent a stylish, fully furnished 2-bed flat in the heart of Brussels for just $221 per night. It's close to De Brouckere metro station, the Opera House, Rue Neuve and Grand Place. It includes a living room, fully equipped kitchen and two bathrooms - plenty of room for a traveling family.

4. Sightseeing

Brussels seems to shrug off its importance as the capital of Belgium and the European Union, and become an easy-going, small city. It's the main educational and economic hub, giving it a more work-a-day feel, as compared to other cities in Europe.

In Brussels, you get a good feel for life in Belgium, particularly its fantastic café and restaurant culture. It doesn't have the star attractions that other towns in Belgium do, but it does have plenty of sights and attractions to keep you busy for three days. You'll enjoy its art galleries and museums, along with the Atomium and old architecture.

Grand Place
This is the main plaza of Brussels Old Town, and is among the best preserved such areas in Europe. A great deal of its elegant character comes from the unique guild house architecture,

with magnificent balustrades, gables and pilasters, rich gold decoration and ornately carved stonework.

Most of the buildings in this area were constructed from 1696 to 1700 in a Baroque style, influenced by Flemish styles. The Grand Place dates back much earlier than that, though. And it has been the economic and political center for Brussels since the 11th century.

Place Royale

This is the most important edifice on the square of Grand Place. It is used as an official residence by the country's royal family. If you're close by at 2:30 pm, you can watch the changing of the guard. Many cultural buildings surround the palace, with elegant neoclassical facades.

Manneken Pis

You're not reading the name of this statue wrong – it translates fairly directly. It's the best-known landmark of Brussels, and it is normally surrounded by tourists. There is not a great deal known regarding the origin of this figure, a little boy urinating.

There are many legends that surround him, though. The current statue was created in 1619, and it has been stolen and recovered several times. During festivals and events in Brussels, he may be seen wearing costumes.

Atomium

This is another famous landmark, and the most surreal attraction in the city. Made from aluminum and steel, it was designed for the World Exhibition in Brussels in 1958. It represents one iron molecule magnified 165 million times. You can enter the landmark, and view a show about the life of humans, called Biogenium.

Place du Châtelain

The Place du Chatelain is the location of the artisan market, held every Wednesday. It's open air shopping at its best. Whether it rains or not, the market stalls brim with delicious food that can be eaten right there.

Into the evening, food shopping changes to a chance to have a plate of snacks and a glass of wine. When night has fallen, the stallholders pack up, and the camaraderie continues in bars on the square's edge, marking the midway point of the work week.

5. Eat & Drink

The cobblestone alleys and historic avenues of Brussels are home to some of the premier dining spots in all of Europe. Since the city is the heart of Europe, it takes advantage of its status and location, serving many cuisines and dishes.

Fine Dining Restaurants

La Villa in the Sky – approximately $412 USD for two

A guide will take you up in the elevator to this glass dining venue. Spectacular meals are served, and the experience is worth the price. The menus change daily, dependent on the in-season produce. Let the server know if you are a vegetarian or vegan, or have allergies or other dietary requirements. You won't be disappointed in the delectable dishes.

Sea Grill – approximately $458 USD for two

The chef at Sea Grill creates magic with seafood and fresh local ingredients. The menu depends on the catch of the day. Their tables are secluded in this Michelin 2-star restaurant. The marriages struck between food and wine are exquisite. The staff serves at a calm pace, right through the wonderful desserts.

Le Chalet de la Forêt – approximately $332 USD for two

You'll remember a meal at Le Chalet for a long time, and cherish each bite. The chef and his team are creative and skillful, and the food is beyond excellent. The staff are attentive, professional and friendly. Try the Brittany lobster with crisp sweetbread, or their Dry, aged Holstein with bone marrow and Agria potato risotto.

San Daniele – approximately $148 USD for two

The service in this restaurant is impeccable and friendly, and the menu is wonderful. The Italian Specialty menu includes Carpaccio, with black truffle. The Tagliolini and truffle are cooked expertly and the cappuccino disappears as soon as it arrives. Dessert is quite special, too, including a pear with a brownie on the bottom.

Mid-range Restaurants

La Quincaillerie – approximately $126 USD for two

This eatery is named for its location in the shop of an ironmonger. The wooden accents and brass elements create a wonderful Art Deco architectural design. The cuisine also combines elegance and tradition. Begin at the oyster bar, then taste painstakingly prepared classics inspired by French cuisine. The ingredients are sourced from local farmers. Among the favorites is the Plate with six rock oysters From Normandie and the Italian beef tartar served with truffle oil and homemade French fries.

Toukoul – approximately $114 USD for two

This cultural house and Ethiopian restaurant is exotic and beautiful, with unique pieces and sculptures directly from Ethiopia. The venue offers weekend concerts of blues, jazz and lounge music.

The sourdough pancake (injera) is the best in town, according to diners. It is topped with spicy sauces. Perhaps you would prefer the succulent, tasty tibs. Tibs are made with fried meat and vegetables with spices, ranging in taste from mild to hot, whichever is your preference. The Addis Flower cocktail is a perennial favorite. Call ahead to book a reservation.

Belga Queen – approximately $92 USD for two

With its marble columns, contemporary sculpture and stained-glass ceilings, Belga Queen is a wonderful example of 19th century Belgian architecture. The sophistication extends to its menu, with seasonal and classic specials.

The seafood platter with oysters is a popular choice, including Malines cockerel on gingerbread and sprinkled with peach syrup. Belga Queen offers dining with opulence, still in the heart of Brussels.

Aglio e Olio – approximately $90 USD for two

This restaurant has an ambiance suitable for intimacy, and wonderful dining choices. The servers are quite attentive without being intrusive. Their beef carpaccio is among the favorites, and the truffle lasagna is unique and tasty. Repeat diners also recommend the seafood linguini.

Cheap Eats

Tapas Y Mas – approximately $18 USD for two

This is a pleasant place for a relaxing dinner. They have excellent beer choices and the staff is helpful and kind. You'll enjoy whatever favorite dish you choose, like the tortilla and Patatas Bravas, served beside other dishes, including shrimp, chicken and calamari.

Publico – approximately $24 USD for two

This restaurant is highly recommended by locals and tourists alike. Their service is excellent, with friendly wait staff and reasonable prices. Try the Ripe steak or Flemish Carbonnades.

Kohinoor – approximately $26 USD for two

For a simple meal, with a helpful and friendly owner, try Kohinoor. They serve traditional and Indian foods, including chicken tikka masala and Poulet tandoori.

King Kong – approximately $35 USD for two

There aren't many places in Brussels where you can get Peruvian food. This restaurant is well-decorated, with a friendly staff. Among the favorites are fried yucca, which is salty, crispy and cooked for just the right time. The ceviche is fresh and tasty, and the roasted chicken is well-marinated, tender and filled with flavor. Try their homemade beer, a light pilsner.

6. Culture and Entertainment

Brussels is a fast paced cultural and business center, but it represents a melting pot of cultures from Europe and beyond. With two city languages, Dutch and French, the city draws from many histories and cultures that make it the city it is today.

Saint-Michel Cathedral
This Gothic styled church was founded in 1225. However, it was not completed until the 1400s. The impressive façade rises above a broad flight of steps, and is crowned with two tall towers. The large interior of the cathedral is furnished lavishly, and home to amazingly beautiful stained-glass windows.

Royal Museums of Fine Arts of Belgium
This museum is among the largest in the world. The collection started in 1797. It has two parts, the Museum of Modern Art and the Museum of Ancient Art. Included in the Ancient Art

Museum are works from Dirk Bouts, Rogier van der Weyden and Petrus Christus. The Modern Art Museum features an engrossing display that makes new works more accessible to the public.

Mini Europe

This interesting park is found in Bruparck, next to Atomium. It features reproductions of monuments found in the EU in a 1:25 scale. About 80 cities and roughly 350 buildings are included. 350,000 people visit the mini park each year.

Belgian Comic Strip Center

The Comic Strip Center is found in a Victor Horta designed 1906 building. It's devoted to comic strip and cartoon history. They have an exhibition that is constantly rotated, with 200 comic strip original drawings by French and Belgian comic artists. They also have a collection of reconstructed sets, original manuscripts and draft sketches.

Brussels Night-Life

Brussels is not a large city, so it doesn't have as many clubs and bars as some bigger European cities. However, from the few excellent clubs, cocktail places and neighborhood bars, they make up what they lack in numbers with class.

Mirano Continental

This dance club is fashion-conscious, but its main attractions are a revolving dance floor and flashing lights. It's a place designed just for carefree fun. Dress to impress and have the cover charge ready if you want to enjoy a night here.

De Ultieme Hallucinate

This is a chic club made in a 1920s train car. The Art Nouveau style really works in this club. The crowd is relatively young, and they enjoy snacking on sandwiches and salads and drinking Belgian brews. In the warmer months, lots of partiers enjoy sipping their drinks on the terrace.

La Fleur en Papier Dore

This club is a hangout for popular music and other artists since its opening. Local writers and poets jot musings on the club's walls. The eclectic décor includes everything from bike tires to antlers. Enjoy a beer and read some of the best works of local artists.

7. Special Events in Brussels

Winter Wonders (after Christmas) January through March

Winter is not the prime time for touring Brussels, but they don't close the city down for the season. On the metro, on foot or by bike, you can wander the winter sights. Ride the big wheel or check out the ice rink. Experience flavors and aromas in the center of town.

Hopla! April

This is the circus arts festival of Brussels. It's held in the second week of Easter holidays. Foreign and Belgian artists perform in cultural centers and public spaces in Brussels. It's free for everyone.

Belgian Pride May

It's not news that Brussels is Belgium's gay capital city. They have a great celebration every summer. Mini Pride kicks off the celebration, followed closely by the Pride Festival. There are many chances to see popular local performers.

Brussels Jazz Marathon   **May**

This free music marathon is the place to be for music lovers. During its run, Brussels is filled with more than 700 artists who perform more than 200 concerts, some indoors, some outdoors. Jazz makes a great soundtrack for sightseeing. You can enjoy the artists in Grand Place, Place Fernand or Place Sainte Catherine, among other venues.

Dinner in the Sky   **June**

This is a chance of a lifetime to enjoy a delicious dinner with just 21 other guests and a world-famous chef in a dining room that is sky high. The vistas of the city and fine dining are a great combination. You'll need to sign up online to be advised when the reservations open.

Tomorrowland   **July**

Belgium welcomes nearly 150,000 visitors to their Tomorrowland festival every year. It's held north of Brussels and celebrates the genre of electronic music. It was once a small festival, drawing just 10,000 visitors, but it is now one of the most popular music festivals in Europe.

Ommegang   June & July

This tradition takes place each year in June and July, in Brussels. Legend says the origin of Ommegang harkens back to a devout local woman who had a vision of the Virgin Mary, telling her to steal a statue in Antwerp and put it in Brussels' Crossbow Guild chapel. As legend has it, the woman was able to steal the statue and bring it by boat to Brussels. An annual procession, "Ommegang", features the statue being carried through Brussels.

Brussels Summer Festival   August

If you're planning a summer visit to Brussels, add this festival to your itinerary. You can see various national entertainers, and enjoy the festivities. Tickets must be booked in advance for this popular event.

Spa GP Formula 1™   August

If you love cars and excitement, come to Brussels in August for the annual Belgian Formula One Grand Prix™. See the best professional drivers test their skills behind the wheel of some of the fastest cars in the world.

Winter Wonders   November-December

This festival brings Brussels alive with holiday spirit. Visiting the Christmas market gives you a chance to slow down your pace and find some unique gifts for your family and friends. There are many booths, filled with exciting finds and local goods.

8. Safety in Brussels

Brussels is indeed a beautiful city for sightseeing, as long as you use common sense and remain vigilant.

Pickpockets

Pickpockets are sometimes an issue in Brussels, as with any crowded, tourist city. It is especially prevalent in touristy areas, and areas that are otherwise crowded. Don't give money to people on the streets. Keep your wallet, camera and phone close to your body. Zippered purses and wallets can help.

After Dark

As in any city, it's a good idea to be cautious when you go out at night. Avoid the Red-Light District (near Gare du Nord Station). It's also a good idea to stay away from bus depots and train stations, to avoid pickpockets.

Taxis

Travelers have warned against a shuttle service named Charleroitransfer. They have missed pickups many times and have inconsistent pricing. When you hail any taxi, confirm the mileage and fare before your ride starts. Note the number on the taxi you take, in case you leave something behind.

Conclusion

If you're planning a trip to Brussels, this book gives you an insight into the best places to stay and eat, and what attractions to make sure you have time to visit. Many travelers don't prepare in advance for their trips, and hope for the best after their arrival. There are amazing places in Brussels, and you don't want to miss the best ones.

We'll let you know where the good places to stay are, what restaurants are the best, which attractions are worth your time and where to party, if you wish. This is not a boring travel guide, because Brussels is not a boring tourist town.

Our goal is to show you the best that Brussels has to offer, so that you can plan ahead and make the most of the few days you have in town. You don't want to miss anything. We'll make sure that doesn't happen.

Printed in Great Britain
by Amazon